A *is for* ALLAH

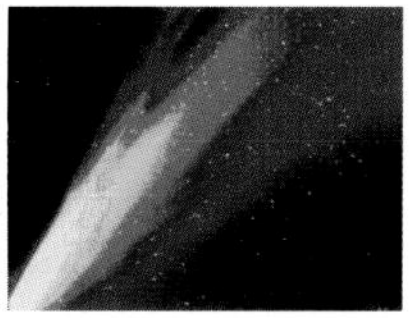

A *is for* ALLAH

YUSUF ISLAM

MOUNTAIN *of* LIGHT

This edition first published in 1999
Reprinted with minor corrections in 2000

Published by Mountain of Light
Mountain of Light Productions Ltd PO Box 7404 London N7 8JQ UK
Mountain of Light South Africa (PTY) LTD PO Box 43486 Industria 2042 South Africa
Astrolabe Islamic Media 201 Davis Dr Suite I Sterling VA 20164 USA

www.mountainoflight.com

British Libary Cataloguing in Publication Data
A catalogue record of this book is available
from The British Library

ISBN 1 900675 31 5

Also available
ISBN 1 900675 28 5 Double CD
ISBN 1 900675 27 7 Double Cassette

Printed in Italy

Table of Contents

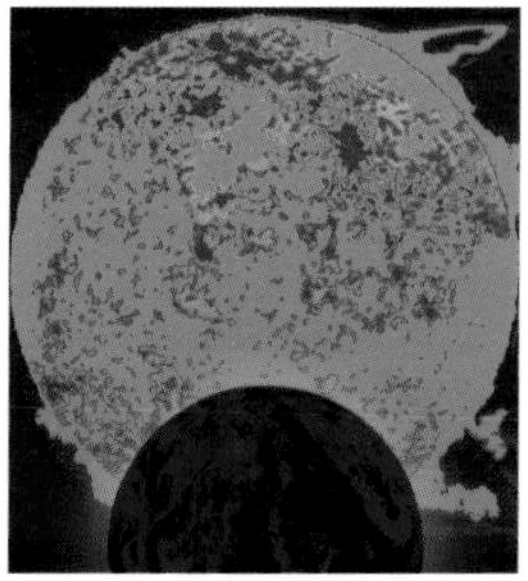

وهذه صورة افلاك القمر وهي مدارات مراكز الاكر التامة على حسب ما تصور على البسط لافهام البراهين
وحساب التعاديل على انا صورنا مثلا التدوير والمدير في ثمانية اماكن وتلك الاماكن هي الاجتماع والاستقبال
والتربيعين وفي
لسهل تصور ذلك

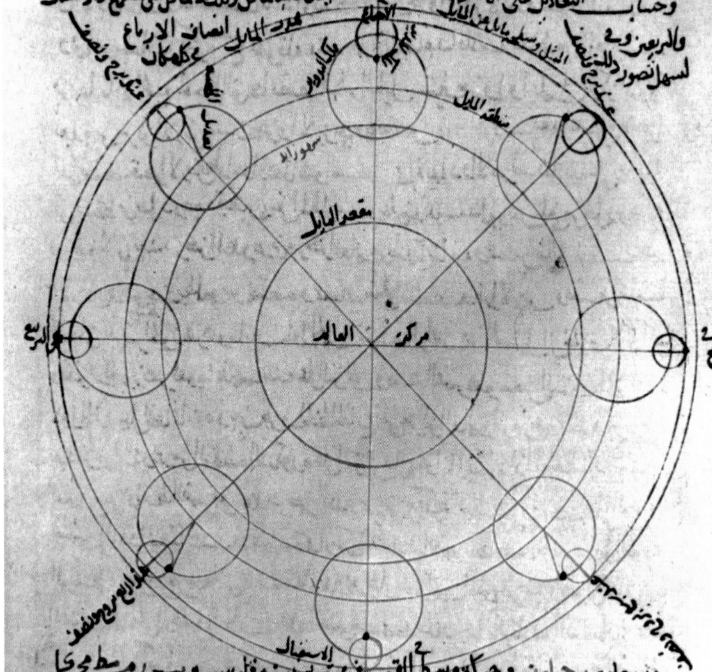

وتسعاية رج له ن وحركة وسط القمر في عشرين سنة فارسية ب رم سط مح كا
وفي سنة واحدة د ط يج ب كط كه الحرقي ثلاثين يوما اه ىرك لو نو ح ط وفي يوم بليلته
يج ى له الحرف لو ح نو ر وفي ساعة مستوية ط ط لب نو كز لم مالا وكتبنا ان
خاصة القمر للتاريخ المذكور دح له كر وحركتها في عشرين سنة فارسية ما د كب ل
وفي سنة واحدة ب ع محر و في شهر اا لو خ وفي يوم ط لح ح يخ توري ساعة ط لب
لمه واثبتنا وسط الجوزهر للتاريخ المذكور ط ه رله وحركته الى خلاف التوالي في عشرين
سنة

Bismillāhi ar-Rahmāni ar-Raheem

All praise belongs to Allah, the Lord of the Worlds - Who taught Adam the names of all things; Who commanded the Angels to bow before Man as a symbol of His Grace, endowing him with the gift of knowledge and Revelation - and peace and blessings of Allah be upon His last Messenger to mankind, Muḥammad, and peace be upon his Family and Companions together.

Introduction

One of the greatest gifts we have been granted is the ability to read, to learn and to follow the Words of guidance sent down to us by Allah, the Lord of the Universe. By understanding His words and message, we are then able to acquire Faith and knowledge of the unseen and to, thereby, understand the original purpose of our existence: to know and worship the One and only God of all Creation.

> I have only created Jinn and men that they may serve Me. [1]

The history of *A is for Allah* spans over two decades. Following the birth of my first child, Hasanah, in 1980, my concern naturally turned towards her education. Realizing the power and influence of the Western culture and education system - having been reared and gone through it myself as a young lad - I knew that this was a major challenge. The philosophy of life which pervades Western society today, begins with the very first lesson a child learns in the classroom; from day one, most children are mechanically programmed to believe that 'A', without question, everlastingly stands for 'Apple'.

The primal etching on the minds of such innocent beings and the attention teachers give to certain things has a long lasting influence on a person's perception of this world. The 'apple' symbolises everything that is delicious: the love, colour and taste of this world (*dunya*) and the gut instinct to satisfy our tummies. But how are we going to fulfil the other basic human desire: the satisfaction of knowing and loving our Creator? I soon realised that my first duty as a parent was to guide my young child in the early and sensitive stages of untainted childhood to understand the Grand Truth behind life and all its wonders and to prepare for everything she was likely to experience as time passes. My intention, therefore, in writing the song, *A is for Allah*, was to teach my daughter that - before all else - 'Alif' [as 'A' is pronounced in Arabic] is for Allah, and that everything else that we love and appreciate in this earthly life, originates from His Divine Will and grace - apples and all.

Many friends and acquaintances assisted me over the years in writing and refining *A is for Allah*, the book. Beginning with Dr Khalid Siddiqi, the first headmaster of Islamia School who, from our London office in Curzon Street, started the initial research on the letters of the Arabic Alphabet and explanations of words from the Qur'an to teacher Tijani Gahbiche, my first esteemed Arabic teacher, who also gave important advice while I was trying to decide which out of hundreds of thousands of Arabic words and phrases to choose. And Hassan Kilgour, an English Muslim who had a special way with words and especially understood the mind frame of children. All these, including my wife, and many more, helped to shape the text, which finally contributed to the book you are about to read.

The design of this book also has its own interesting tale. Just after I embraced Islam, I bumped into a fellow musician who had also become Muslim a year or so before me, Ian Whiteman. He had adopted the name 'Abd al-Lateef and was working as a designer at the time. 'Abd al-Lateef could also write Arabic calligraphy and displayed a distinctive flair with the pen. I introduced him to *A is for Allah* and in an early letter to him dated 16th September 1981, wrote: *'Here is the Islamic Alphabet I said I'd send you. I have coloured some letters, but this is just rough, and I'm sure there will be quite a few changes before it's done'*. A truer word could not have been said. Almost twenty years later, we finally managed to complete the book! Much of the beauty in the design is due to his masterful style and talent. May Allah Almighty, in Whose name we began this work, reward him and everyone else who helped in its development and accomplishment.

I pray that *A is for Allah* will succeed in inspiring young hearts to enrich their knowledge of Islam and learn the skill of reading the Book of Life itself, the miracles of which are all around us, if we but realised. As Allah Almighty says in the Qur'an,

> Among His signs are the Sun and the Moon. Adore not the Sun nor the Moon, but adore Allah Who created them if it is Him you wish to serve.[2]

YUSUF ISLAM 1420H/1999CE

1 Sūrah al-Dhāriyāt (51): 56   2 Sūrah Fuṣṣilat (41): 37

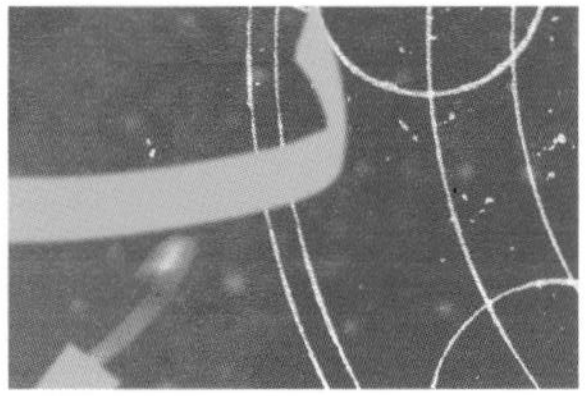

ا is for Allah, nothing but Allah

ب is the beginning of Bismillāh

ت is for Taqwā, bewaring of Allah

ث is for Thawāb, a Reward

ج is for Jannah, the Garden of Paradise

ح is for Ḥajj, The Blessed Pilgrimage

خ is for Khātam, the Seal of the Prophethood given to the Prophet Muḥammad (ṣalla Allāhu ʻalayhi wa sallam)

د is for Deen, al-Islām, religion with Allah since time began

ذ is for Dhikr, remembering Allah

ر is for the month of Ramaḍān

ز is for Zakāh, to cure our greed when we give our money to those in need

س is for Salāmun ʻalaykum (peace be with you) wa ʻalaykumu as-salām

ش is for Shams, the shining sun, which Allah placed for everyone

ص is for Ṣalāh, for when we pray facing Him everyday, facing him till we meet our Lord.

Allah, there's only one God, and Muḥammad is His Messenger. Allah, lā ilāha illa-Allāh

ض is for Ḍuḥā, the morning light, the sun has turned from red to white

ط is for Ṭareeq, a path to walk on

ظ is for Ẓill, a shadow

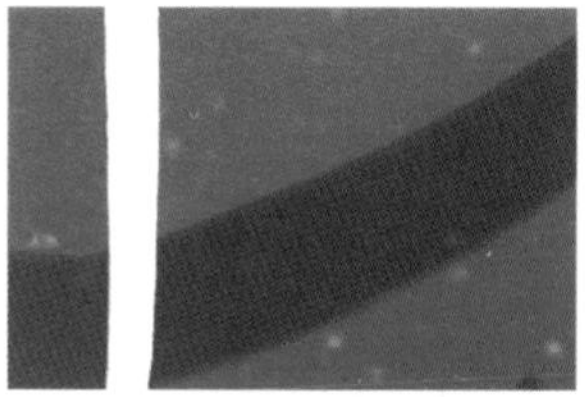

ع is for ʻIlm, the thing to know, to make our knowledge grow in Islam

غ is for Ghayb, a world unseen, and that we know is not a dream

ف is for the Opening, al-Fātiḥah

ق is for the Qur'an, the Book of God

ك is for Kalimah, a Word we're taught, to teach us what is good and what is not

ل is for the beginning of: lā ilāha illa-Allāh

م is for the Messenger: Muḥammadun Rasūl-Allāh, lā ilāha illa-Allāh, Muḥammadun Rasūl-Allāh
Allah, there's only one God, and Muḥammad is His Messenger. Allah, lā ilāha illa-Allāh

ن is for Nawm, the sleep God gave, to give us rest after the day

ه is for the Hijrah, the Journey that the Prophet made

و for Wuḍū' before we pray, to help us wash our sins away

ي is for Yawm ad-Deen

Allah, there's only one God, and Muḥammad is His Messenger, Allah, lā ilāha illa-Allāh
Allah, there's only one God, and Jesus was His Messenger, Allah, lā ilāha illa-Allāh
Allah, there's only one God, and Moses was His Messenger, Allah, lā ilāha illa-Allāh
Allah, there's only one God, and Abraham was His Messenger, Allah, lā ilāha illa-Allāh
Allah, there's only one God, and Noah was His Messenger, Allah, lā ilāha illa-Allāh
Allah, there's only one God, and He created Adam, and we are the children of Adam,
Allah, lā ilāha illa-Allāh

ALLAH

Allah is the proper name for God, the Lord of the universe. He was not born and has no child so we cannot compare Him to anything else: that is because He is Allah, the Maker and Creator of everything. He does not need to sleep nor rest and though we cannot see Him, yet He sees us; and He knows every little thing going on in the heavens and the earth.

Allah is the Most Kind, the Most Loving. He has given us everything that we have: He gives us water, food, light, air and all that we need to live on this earth until the day we die. He gave us minds and hearts so as to see how much we are thankful through worshipping and obeying Him; so pleasing Allah with our faith and good behaviour should be the main aim of our life.

We can only get to know Him through His own Words and Guidance to us: so let's now turn to the Book of Allah, to *Āyatu-al-Kursī* – the Verse of the Throne:

ٱللَّهُ لَآ إِلَٰهَ إِلَّا هُوَ
ٱلْحَىُّ ٱلْقَيُّومُ ۚ لَا تَأْخُذُهُۥ سِنَةٌ وَلَا نَوْمٌ ۚ لَّهُۥ مَا فِى ٱلسَّمَٰوَٰتِ وَمَا
فِى ٱلْأَرْضِ ۗ مَن ذَا ٱلَّذِى يَشْفَعُ عِندَهُۥٓ إِلَّا بِإِذْنِهِۦ ۚ يَعْلَمُ مَا بَيْنَ
أَيْدِيهِمْ وَمَا خَلْفَهُمْ ۖ وَلَا يُحِيطُونَ بِشَىْءٍ مِّنْ عِلْمِهِۦٓ إِلَّا بِمَا
شَآءَ ۚ وَسِعَ كُرْسِيُّهُ ٱلسَّمَٰوَٰتِ وَٱلْأَرْضَ ۖ وَلَا يَـُٔودُهُۥ حِفْظُهُمَا ۚ
وَهُوَ ٱلْعَلِىُّ ٱلْعَظِيمُ

Allah,
there is no god but He, the Living,
the Self-Sustaining.
No slumber can seize Him, nor sleep.
His are all things in the heavens and on earth.
Who can mediate with Him, except by His permission? He knows whatever was before them and whatever shall come after them; and they do not encompass anything of His knowledge except as He wills. His Throne extends over the heavens and the earth, and He feels no tiredness in guarding them; for He is the High, the Supreme.

[Sūrah al-Baqarah (2): 255]

" Say He is Allah, the only One; we all need Him and He needs no one; He has no parents, no daughter, no son; Nobody is like Him and He is like no one; Say He is Allah, the only One."

Allah has sent Prophets and Messengers to speak His Words to us, reminding us to worship only Him and to show us how to live properly, following His Guidance. One Day, when He commands, the heavens will split, stars and planets will fall apart and the world will come to an end. After this, Allah the Almighty will raise us all back to life again, to be judged and rewarded or punished for what we have done. People who worshipped false gods or other things will be very sorry on that Day, but those who listened to Allah and did good will be the happiest of all.

ب

BISMILLĀH

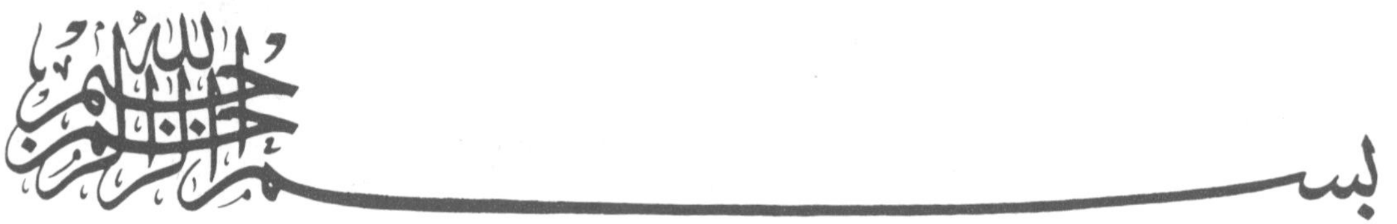

Bada'na Bismillāh
wa bi-ṣalāti-Allāh
'Alā Rasūl-Allāh
Wa ālihi al-abrār

Begin with Bismilllāh
and with Salāt-Allāh
upon Rasūl-Allāh
and his righteous family

Bismillāh means 'In the Name of Allah', these are the first words which begin the Glorious Qur'an. Muslims are taught to mention the name of Allah whenever beginning anything. This is so we always remember Him and know that we need His permission and help in everything that we do.

It is good to remember to say *Bismillāhi ar-Rahmāni ar-Raheem* before eating, washing, starting a journey or beginning any job. If, for instance, we say *Bismillāh* before eating, it helps us to realise that food comes from plants and animals which were created by Allah; they drank water from the rain that He sends down, warmed by the bright Sun that He causes to rise: all this is done in order to give us the food which our bodies need. So by saying *Bismillāh*, we show that we are thankful for Allah's mercy, by guiding us and keeping us alive and healthy.

TAQWĀ

ت

Taqwā means righteousness or, as it is sometimes called, Fear of Allah. When someone has *Taqwā* it means he is always careful to say and do the right things: like a person walking through a forest filled with thorns, he will try not to get hurt or scratched.

People with *Taqwā* are those who realise that Allah knows and sees everything that they do, whether good or bad, so they are always careful to try and behave in the right way. They believe in the unseen, perform their prayers and spend in charity. They keep their promises and are patient, even in times of great pain and trouble. They know that the life after death is real; so they beware of the dangers of this world and prepare for the true dawn of tomorrow.

يَٰٓأَيُّهَا ٱلَّذِينَ ءَامَنُوا۟ ٱتَّقُوا۟ ٱللَّهَ
وَلْتَنظُرْ نَفْسٌ مَّا قَدَّمَتْ لِغَدٍ ۖ
وَٱتَّقُوا۟ ٱللَّهَ ۚ إِنَّ ٱللَّهَ خَبِيرٌۢ بِمَا
تَعْمَلُونَ

Oh you who believe!
Fear Allah and let every soul look to what it sends forth for tomorrow and beware of Allah; verily Allah is aware of what you do.

[Sūrah al-Ḥashr (59):18]

ث

THAWĀB

Thawāb means a 'reward', it is a payment for some kind of work done. If your parents asked you to do a special job for them, and you did it very well, they might give you a reward. Allah the Almighty also gives rewards for good deeds, but His rewards are the greatest we could ever dream of!

The most wonderful *thawāb* we can be given is to live forever in Paradise after we die, and this is the reward that a good Muslim works for in this life. A true believer will not waste his time in this world only counting his wealth or his children. Many Muslims in the past, and even right up to today, have suffered because of their faith in the truth of Islam, however, they are still happy to be Muslims and are full of hope. They know that no matter how much they suffer in this world, it could never be as bad as the punishment in the Hereafter for those who disobey their Lord.

In order to be rewarded with a good life for Eternity we must do good deeds and obey Allah and His Messenger, *ṣalla Allāhu 'alayhi wa sallam*; this is the hope for the best *thawāb.*

ٱلْمَالُ وَٱلْبَنُونَ زِينَةُ
ٱلْحَيَوٰةِ ٱلدُّنْيَا ۖ
وَٱلْبَـٰقِيَـٰتُ ٱلصَّـٰلِحَـٰتُ
خَيْرٌ عِندَ رَبِّكَ
ثَوَابًا وَخَيْرٌ أَمَلًا

Wealth and children are ornaments of the life of the world, but the good deeds which last, are best with your Lord as reward; and (your) best hope.

[Sūrah al-Kahf (18): 46]

JANNAH

Jannah means Garden – it means the Garden of Paradise: a place where all wishes come true. No one has to work or suffer in *Jannah*; it isn't like here on earth where many people have a hard life and are treated cruelly by others. In *Jannah* everyone is kind and enjoys an easy, happy life that goes on forever without end.

Jannah is prepared for a special kind of people, not everyone may enter. So we have to work very hard in this life and try our best to follow the Truth and avoid evil.

It is very important for Muslims to remember that being happy here on earth is not everything. Many people in the world today do not believe in the unseen so they think that the most important thing is to have a good time before they die. Of course, everyone would like to be always having fun in this life, but it is much more important to prepare for the Hereafter. We only live on this earth for a little while and, as much as you try, you can never imagine being as happy here as you would be in Paradise, where everything will be, forever and always, just the way you want it.

ج

In the Qur'an, in Sūrah *al-Kahf*, Allah Almighty promises His believing servants *Jannah*:

أُولَٰئِكَ لَهُمْ جَنَّٰتُ عَدْنٍ تَجْرِي مِن تَحْتِهِمُ
الْأَنْهَٰرُ يُحَلَّوْنَ فِيهَا مِنْ أَسَاوِرَ مِن ذَهَبٍ
وَيَلْبَسُونَ ثِيَابًا خُضْرًا مِّن سُندُسٍ وَإِسْتَبْرَقٍ
مُّتَّكِـِٔينَ فِيهَا عَلَى الْأَرَآئِكِ ۚ نِعْمَ الثَّوَابُ
وَحَسُنَتْ مُرْتَفَقًا

For them will be Gardens of Eternity; beneath them rivers will flow: they will be adorned therein with bracelets of gold and they will wear green garments of silk and heavy brocade. They will recline therein on raised thrones. How blissful is the reward and how beautiful

Labbaik, Allahumma labbaik, labbaik, lā shareeka laka labbaik, inna al-Hamda wa-an-ni'mata laka wa al-Mulk, lā shareeka lak. Labbaik, Allāhumma labbaik, labbaik, lā shareeka laka la

ح

ḤAJJ

To make *Ḥajj* is to travel and visit the House of Allah in Makkah and surrounding areas on Pilgrimage. It is one of the five pillars of Islam, so every grown up Muslim must make *Ḥajj* at least once during their lifetime, as long as they can afford to and are healthy enough.

Ḥajj is the biggest and most wonderful gathering of people on earth. It was started thousands of years ago by the Prophet Ibrahim and his first son, Isma'il, *'alayhima as-Salām*. Every year, during the holy month of *Ḥajj* (called *Dhu al-Ḥijjah*), people come to the same place, wearing the same clothes, say the same words and worship in the same way; it is the greatest show of the oneness of mankind in the world. Millions of people arrive from many far and distant lands; they are different colours and speak different languages, but they are all believers and servants of the One Lord. Therefore, they all come as brothers and sisters and stand equal before Him.

-Hamda wa-an-ni'mata laka wa al-Mulk, lā shareeka lak. Labbaik, Allahumma labbaik, labbaik, lā shareeka laka labbaik, inna al-Hamda wa-an-ni'mata laka wa al-Mulk, lā shareeka lak.

When Muslims make the Pilgrimage to the House, they have to do special things, like the *Ṭawāf* – going seven times around the Holy Ka'bah; and walking between the two small hills of *aṣ-Ṣafā* and *al-Marwah*. Then, after spending a night nearby in Minā, on the ninth day of the month the *Ḥājjīs* gather to stand on the open fields of 'Arafah, calling and praying to their Lord, until sunset. This is the great day of *Ḥajj:* the day of forgiveness and mercy. On the morning of the tenth day, after dawn prayer, the pilgrims return to Minā to throw pebbles at the three big stone pillars.[1] After this they sacrifice an animal, in memory of the Prophet Ibrahim and his willingness to sacrifice his beloved son, Isma'il. The pilgrims stay in Minā to throw pebbles again at the three stone pillars and make their final rounds of the Ka'bah for the last time.

Performing *Ḥajj* is a very important duty for Muslims. The Prophet Muḥammad, *ṣalla Allāhu 'alayhi wa sallam*, said,

'If anyone makes the pilgrimage for Allah's sake, without talking sinfully or acting badly, then that person will return as free from sin as the day his mother gave birth to him'.[2]

1 Starting with only the largest pillar on the tenth day and followed by all three pillars on the eleventh and twelfth days 2 Al-Bukhari and Muslim

خ

KHĀTAM

Khātam means a seal. The Prophet Muḥammad, *ṣalla Allāhu 'alayhi wa sallam*, is known as the Seal of the Prophets; meaning that he was the 'last' of the Prophets.

Today, if we want to send an important letter, we put it inside an envelope and close the envelope by sealing it so it cannot be opened except by tearing it. In the old days there were no paper envelopes. When a letter was written and completed, it was rolled up and a drop of wax stuck down the edge. Then a signet ring – a ring with a name on it – was pressed into the wax while still soft, leaving a print of the name and sealing the letter. The dried seal showed that the letter was now finished and could not be changed.

Allah Almighty has sent many Prophets to mankind to deliver His message and to show people how to live in the way that He wishes. He made the Religion complete by choosing the Prophet Muḥammad, *ṣalla Allāhu 'alayhi wa sallam*, as His last Prophet. Nothing can be added or taken away because it has now been finished and sealed.

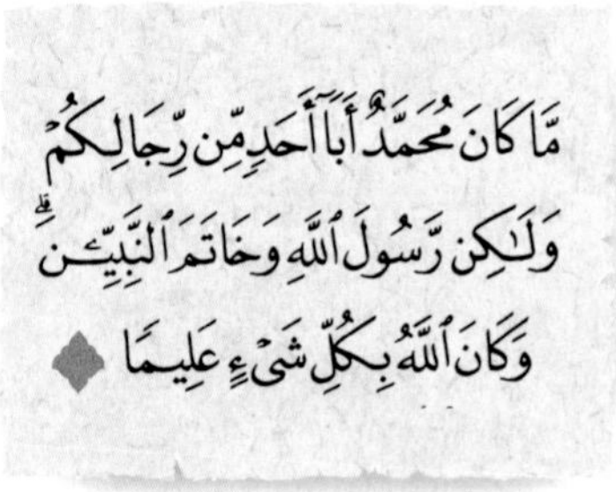
مَّا كَانَ مُحَمَّدٌ أَبَآ أَحَدٍ مِّن رِّجَالِكُمْ
وَلَٰكِن رَّسُولَ ٱللَّهِ وَخَاتَمَ ٱلنَّبِيِّـۧنَ
وَكَانَ ٱللَّهُ بِكُلِّ شَىْءٍ عَلِيمًا

Muḥammad is not the father of any one of your men, but he is the Messenger of Allah and the Seal of the Prophets: and Allah has full knowledge of all things.

[Sūrah al-Aḥzāb (33): 40]

يا أيها النبي إنا أرسلناك شاهدا ومبشرا ونذيرا وداعيا إلى الله

د DEEN

Deen means the complete way of life given to us by our Creator, Allah, through the teachings of the Prophets. This guidance has been sent to us so that we may live in the right way while we are here on earth. For Muslims, the *Deen* covers all sides of life, it is not just a 'religion' only for our spiritual needs. We are taught everything, from the right way to eat or keep ourselves clean, to the best way to run a country, or look after the earth.

The *Deen* is based on belief. There are six most important things that a Muslim must believe in:

- ALLAH
- HIS ANGELS
- HIS BOOKS
- HIS MESSENGERS
- THE LAST DAY
- QADAR (whatever Allah has decided, both good and bad)

After believing, a Muslim must also do the right things. The main duties of a Muslim are sometimes called the Five Pillars of Islam. They are:

- ASH-SHAHĀDAH – openly say that there is no God but Allah and that Muḥammad is His Messenger
- AṢ-ṢALĀH – making five daily prayers
- AZ-ZAKĀH – giving some of your wealth to needy people
- AṢ-ṢAWM – fasting during the month of Ramaḍān
- AL-ḤAJJ – making at least one pilgrimage to Makkah, if you are able to

These things are at the heart of the Islamic way of life. But Muslims should also look into the life of the Prophet Muḥammad, *ṣalla Allāhu ʻalayhi wa sallam*, to find out what he had to say about all kinds of everyday matters and to see how he lived. By following his *Sunnah* – or living example – we find out how to follow the way of life that Allah has taught us.

Dustūruna al-Qur'ānu wa Deenuna al-Islam; Arkānuhu al-Jaleelah, dā'iman faḍeelah; wa hiya ash-Shahādatāni qā'idatu al-Imāni; Wa aṣ-Ṣawmu wa aṣ-Ṣalātu, wa al-Ḥajju wa az-Zakātu.

Our guide is the Qur'an, our Religion is Islam; Five noble pillars upholding what is virtuous; To make the Testimony is the base of the Faith; And the Fast and the Prayer, the Pilgrimage and Charity.

سورة
يس

DHIKR

ذ

Dhikr is remembering – it means remembering Allah. The best thing would be to remember Allah as if you were seeing Him, but even though you cannot see Him, to know that He is seeing you is the best way to remember.

It may be difficult for us to keep Allah in our thoughts all the time because we are easily carried away by the things going on around us; if we forget, we can easily go astray and do things which are wrong. By remembering Allah we know that He is near us, and when we don't remember this, we become unhappy. The Prophet Muḥammad, *ṣalla Allāhu 'alayhi wa sallam*, said, 'Be mindful of Allah, and Allah will protect you. Be mindful of Allah, and you will find Him in front of you…' [3]

The Prophet has taught us how best to remember Allah. We say *Bismillāh* (In the Name of Allah), when starting anything; *al-Ḥamdulillāh* (Praise be to Allah), at any time or when enjoying something; *Inshā'Allāh* (If Allah wishes), when planning about the future; and *A'ūdhu billāh* (I seek protection with Allah), when seeing something nasty or having a nightmare. There are so many ways of remembering – even in your actions – just by obeying Allah in whatever you do.

3 At-Tirmidhee, an-Nawawī's Forty Ḥadeeths, no.19

RAMAḌĀN

Ramaḍān is the name of the ninth month of the Islamic moon calendar. It is very important because it is the month in which the Glorious Qur'an was first sent down by Allah to the Prophet Muḥammad, *ṣalla Allāhu 'alayhi wa sallam*. During *Ramaḍān*, Muslims must fast: we don't eat or drink between dawn and sunset and we should be very careful to speak and behave in the right way.

We learn many things from fasting during *Ramaḍān*. It is a time to increase our remembrance of Allah and remember the blessings which we have been given; we learn how to be thankful for the good things that we normally take for granted. After fasting all day we realise just how wonderful food and drink taste, so we thank Allah more sincerely for providing us with enough to eat and satisfy our thirst.

Ramaḍān is a good form of training. There may come moments or times in life when things are not easy and we have to carry on even though it is difficult. By fasting, we learn to be

patient at such times and to control ourselves and our bodies – this is called 'self-discipline'. During this holy month, the Prophet, *ṣalla Allāhu 'alayhi wa sallam*, said, 'The doors of Heaven are opened, the doors of Hell closed and the devils are chained.'[4]

This helps us to see ourselves as we really are, not under the influence of unseen evil forces. We can watch and improve ourselves more, especially by reading the Qur'an and going to the mosque, joining in the *Tarāweeḥ* prayers. In *Ramaḍān* there is a special night that is better than one thousand months. It is called, *Laylat al-Qadr*: the night in which the Qur'an was first revealed, a night in which all our sins can be forgiven.

Fasting is also important because it makes the rich equal to the poor: it gives them a chance to realise what life is like for the less fortunate, those who have little or no food. This helps them become more charitable and give generously of their wealth to the needy, so that they too can enjoy and share the blessings of Allah which are enough for all.

4 Ahmad and an-Nisā'ī (Mishkāt al-Maṣābeeḥ, vol. 3, ch. 35, p. 515)

وَالَّذِينَ يَكْنِزُونَ الذَّهَبَ
وَالْفِضَّةَ وَلَا يُنْفِقُونَهَا فِي سَبِيلِ اللَّهِ
فَبَشِّرْهُمْ بِعَذَابٍ أَلِيمٍ ◇
يَوْمَ يُحْمَى عَلَيْهَا فِي نَارِ جَهَنَّمَ
فَتُكْوَى بِهَا جِبَاهُهُمْ وَجُنُوبُهُمْ
وَظُهُورُهُمْ هَذَا مَا كَنَزْتُمْ
لِأَنْفُسِكُمْ فَذُوقُوا مَا كُنْتُمْ تَكْنِزُونَ ◆

ZAKĀH

ز

Zakāh means purification in Arabic. To purify something means to make it clean and more pure. Giving *Zakāh* is the best way to purify the money that we have by giving some of it to the poor. Money and valuables are gifts from Allah the Almighty, but some people become greedy when they become rich. They feel proud of themselves, thinking that they have been very clever to make so much money; these people forget that they owe their wealth to Allah. A good Muslim would not think this way, he would know that all things come from Allah and that he must share part of his good fortune with the poor and needy by paying his *Zakāh*. *Zakāh* is so important that it is one of the Five Pillars in Islam; it is an act of worship. It must be paid by those Muslims who have more money saved up at the end of the year than they need to spend. Two and a half per cent, or in other words one part in every forty of their personal savings – money, gold or silver – must be paid as *Zakāh*. Farmers and landowners with cattle or crops have to pay slightly more. However, no matter how much a person may spend in *Zakāh* or charity, they will always be surprised to find that their wealth never goes down. Allah the Almighty will make sure that their provision increases even more. As the Prophet, *ṣalla Allāhu 'alayhi wa sallam*, said, 'Charity taken from property never lessens it.'[5]

For those who do not pay *Zakāh*, there is a harsh warning of severe punishment in the Hereafter – as Allah the Almighty says in the Qur'an:

> ...And those who treasure gold and silver and spend it not in the way of Allah: give them the news of a most grievous punishment. On the Day when heat will be produced from that wealth in the fire of Hell, and it will be branded on their foreheads, their sides and their backs: This is what you treasured for yourselves; then taste, (the wealth) which you hoarded.

[Sūrah at-Tawbah (9): 34-35]

5 At-Tirmidhee, (also Fiqh as-Sunnah vol. 3: Zakāh p. 2)

س

SALĀM

As-Salām is one of the beautiful names of Allah meaning the Owner, or Giver of Peace; it also means that He is Perfect – free from faults or weaknesses. In Arabic, the word *Salām* itself comes from *Sa-li-ma* which means to be 'safe' or 'at peace'. Peace is something that most people dream of in this world; it's something that we wish and pray for in the life to come.

Muslims are taught to greet each other with the words, *'As-Salāmu 'alaykum'*, meaning 'Peace be with you', this is one of the ways we can spread love and peace amongst each other. The Prophet, *ṣalla Allahu 'alayhi wa sallam*, said, 'You will not enter the Garden of Paradise until you believe; and you shall not (truly) believe until you love one another. Shall I guide you to a thing that when you practice it will cause you to love one another? Spread *as-Salām* between yourselves'.[6] The word 'Islam' comes from the same root as *salām* meaning, 'submission'; it means submission to the Will of Allah. Islam is the way to enter into peace and safety. By following the straight path we have been promised to enter into *'Dar as-Salām'* – the everlasting Home of Peace.

6 Ṣaḥeeḥ Muslim (also Mishkāt al-Maṣābeeḥ vol. I, ch. 3, no. 62, p. 293)

Salāmun, salāmun, salāmun, salām. Salāmun, salāmun, salāmun, salām.
Salāmun, salāmun, salāmun, salām. Salāmun, salāmun, salāmun, salām.
Ja'alnā as-salāma shi'ārun lanā; wa bismi as-salāmi at-Taqaynā hunā.
Le taj'ala yā Rabbu ayyāmanā 'alā hādhihi al-Ardi bushra salām
Peaceful, peaceful peaceful peace. Peaceful, peaceful peaceful peace.
Peaceful, peaceful peaceful peace. Peaceful, peaceful peaceful peace.
We made peace a symbol of ours; in the name of peace we gather here now.
O Lord! please make these days of ours on this earth filled with peace.
Salāmun, salāmun, salāmun, salām. Salāmun, salāmun, salāmun, salām.
Salāmun, salāmun, salāmun, salām. Salāmun, salāmun, salāmun, salām.
Fa yā Rabbu innaka anta as-Salām; wa minka as-Salāmu wa 'indaka as-Salām.
Li amrika yarji'u amru al-anām, wa bayna yadayka qulubu al-Anām.
Peaceful, peaceful peaceful peace. Peaceful, peaceful peaceful peace.
Peaceful, peaceful peaceful peace. Peaceful, peaceful peaceful peace.
So Lord, indeed! You are as-Salām, from You comes Salām and with You is Salām.
To You belongs the command of all things; between Your hands
are the hearts of all beings
Peaceful, peaceful peaceful peace. Peaceful, peaceful peaceful peace.
Salāmun, salāmun, salāmun, salām. Salāmun, salāmun, salāmun, salām.
Salāmun, salāmun, salāmun, salām. Salāmun, salāmun, salāmun, salām.

7 Ṣaḥeeḥ Muslim

The Prophet also taught us this prayer:
Allāhumma Anta as-Salāmu, wa minka as-Salāmu, Tabārakta yā dha al-Jalāli wa al-Ikrām

O Allah! You are the Giver of Peace, from You comes peace; Blessed are You, o Possessor of Majesty and Honour [7]

ش SHAMS

The word *Shams* means Sun in Arabic. The Sun is one of the creations of Allah, *subḥānahu wa ta ʿālā*; it is one of His Signs. Allah created the Sun to provide light and heat to all the creatures of this world. It also tells us the time: even without the invention of mechanical clocks and digital watches, it is easy for people to know what hour of the day it is by the settings and shadows of the sun. It is so important that without it, it would be impossible for us to live here on earth: no plants could grow, no rain would fall, no wind would blow. There would be no days, no colours – even the moon would be cloaked in darkness and everything would freeze and die.

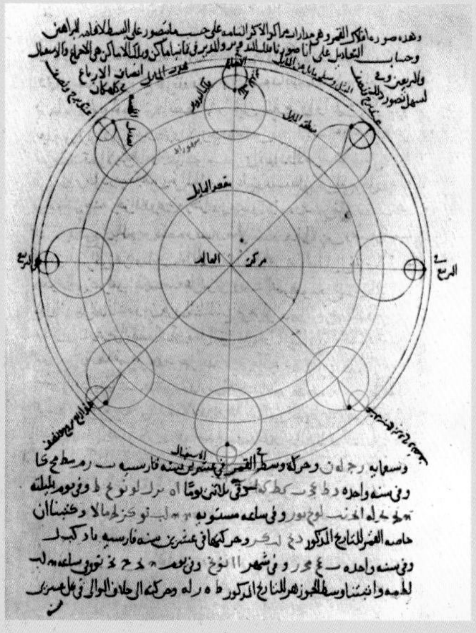

The Sun, because of its importance to human life, has often been looked up to as a great symbol of power and glory; so much so, some people even went as far as to bow down and start worshipping it like a god! But Muslims know that it is only a creation of Allah, it does only what Allah commands it to do; and will shine as long as Allah wants it to.

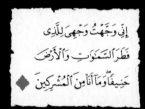

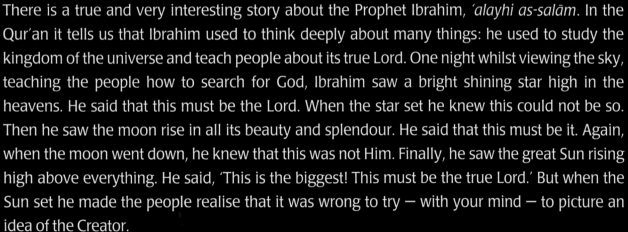

There is a true and very interesting story about the Prophet Ibrahim, *'alayhi as-salām*. In the Qur'an it tells us that Ibrahim used to think deeply about many things: he used to study the kingdom of the universe and teach people about its true Lord. One night whilst viewing the sky, teaching the people how to search for God, Ibrahim saw a bright shining star high in the heavens. He said that this must be the Lord. When the star set he knew this could not be so. Then he saw the moon rise in all its beauty and splendour. He said that this must be it. Again, when the moon went down, he knew that this was not Him. Finally, he saw the great Sun rising high above everything. He said, 'This is the biggest! This must be the true Lord.' But when the Sun set he made the people realise that it was wrong to try – with your mind – to picture an idea of the Creator.

Then he said:

إِنِّي وَجَّهْتُ وَجْهِيَ لِلَّذِي
فَطَرَ ٱلسَّمَٰوَٰتِ وَٱلْأَرْضَ
حَنِيفًا وَمَآ أَنَا۠ مِنَ ٱلْمُشْرِكِينَ ◆

For me, I have set my face towards the One Who created the heavens and the earth, firmly and truly; and I am not of those who make partners (with Him).

[Sūrah al-An'ām (6): 79]

ص ṢALĀH

Ṣalāh is the act of Prayer in Islam. The first duty of every Muslim who believes in Allah and His Messenger is to make *aṣ-Ṣalāh*: the five daily prayers. It involves standing, bowing, prostrating – with your head to the ground – and kneeling. The *Ṣalāh* helps us to remember Allah throughout the day and reminds us that we are His servants, ready to submit and follow His commands.

When we begin *Ṣalāh,* we turn away from the world, leave behind whatever we are doing and think about His greatness. We say *'Allāhu Akbar'* which means 'Allah is the Greatest'. The *Ṣalāh* prayer is also the best time to open up our hearts and speak directly to our Lord. The Prophet, *ṣalla Allāhu 'alayhi wa sallam*, said, 'The closest a servant can be to his Lord is when he is prostrating (head to the ground).’ [8]

The times of the *Ṣalāh* prayers are set by the Sun’s clock: the *Fajr*, begins at dawn before the sun rises; *Ẓuhr*, begins just after it has reached the highest point; *‘Aṣr*, is in the middle of the afternoon; *Maghrib*, comes immediately after the sun has gone down; and *‘Ishā*, is when its red light disappears into the blackness of the night. These are the five main prayers that we should try to pray together – in the Mosque if we can. Of course, before we pray, we must first make sure that we are pure and clean; then we stand shoulder to shoulder in straight lines facing Makkah and follow the Imam. Reading the Qur’an – especially *‘Al-Fātiḥah’*, the first chapter – is a very important part of the *Ṣalāh* prayer; in it we praise and thank Allah, the most Merciful, the most Kind, asking for His guidance both in good times and bad.

The prayers help us to stay close to Allah Almighty and to keep away from evil. Because the prayers are spread throughout the day, even if we do something wrong, we may stop and pray for Allah’s forgiveness and put things right again. One of the biggest sins is for a Muslim to leave *Ṣalāh* altogether: the Prophet, *ṣalla Allāhu ‘alayhi wa sallam*, warned about such a person when he said, ‘Whoever gives it up becomes a disbeliever.’ [9] So, as believers, we should always be careful about making our prayers at the right time.

وَأَقِمِ ٱلصَّلَوٰةَ طَرَفَيِ ٱلنَّهَارِ
وَزُلَفًا مِّنَ ٱلَّيْلِ ۚ إِنَّ ٱلْحَسَنَٰتِ
يُذْهِبْنَ ٱلسَّيِّـَٔاتِ ۚ ذَٰلِكَ
ذِكْرَىٰ لِلذَّٰكِرِينَ

And establish regular prayers at the two ends of the day and at the approaches of the night: for those things that are good remove those that are evil: that is a reminder for the mindful.

[Sūrah Hūd (11): 114]

8 Ṣaḥeeḥ Muslim 9 Aḥmad, at-Tirmidhee, an-Nisā’i and Ibn Mājah (also Mishkāt al-Maṣābeeḥ, vol. 3, ch. 34, p. 161)

ض ḌUḤĀ

بِسۡمِ ٱللَّهِ ٱلرَّحۡمَٰنِ ٱلرَّحِيمِ

وَٱلضُّحَىٰ ◇ وَٱلَّيۡلِ إِذَا سَجَىٰ ◇

مَا وَدَّعَكَ رَبُّكَ وَمَا قَلَىٰ ◇

وَلَلۡأٓخِرَةُ خَيۡرٞ لَّكَ مِنَ ٱلۡأُولَىٰ ◇

وَلَسَوۡفَ يُعۡطِيكَ رَبُّكَ فَتَرۡضَىٰٓ ◇

أَلَمۡ يَجِدۡكَ يَتِيمٗا فَـَٔاوَىٰ ◇

وَوَجَدَكَ ضَآلّٗا فَهَدَىٰ ◇

وَوَجَدَكَ عَآئِلٗا فَأَغۡنَىٰ ◇

فَأَمَّا ٱلۡيَتِيمَ فَلَا تَقۡهَرۡ ◇

وَأَمَّا ٱلسَّآئِلَ فَلَا تَنۡهَرۡ ◇

وَأَمَّا بِنِعۡمَةِ رَبِّكَ فَحَدِّثۡ ◆

Ḍuḥā means the 'forenoon'; that time of day after the sun has risen in the bright mid-morning hours, before it gets too hot. The Prophet, *ṣalla Allāhu 'alayhi wa sallam*, used to offer special prayers at this time. Sūrah *aḍ-Ḍuḥā* is also the name of a chapter of the Qur'an: some say it was the third one to be revealed by Allah Almighty to the Prophet Muḥammad, *ṣalla Allāhu 'alayhi wa sallam*. This Sūrah came after a long gap during which he received no revelation at all; this was a worrying time for the Prophet, *ṣalla Allāhu 'alayhi wa sallam*, and he probably felt very sad and lonely. Not many people had accepted Allah's message at that time of his mission and those who didn't believe in it were pleased to see him receiving no guidance. They made cruel jokes and mocked him. The wife of Abu Lahab [the uncle and enemy of our Prophet, *ṣalla Allāhu 'alayhi wa sallam*] told him, 'I think your satan has left you.'

So Sūrah *aḍ-Ḍuḥā* arrived like glorious sunshine after a cold, dark night. In it, Allah Almighty tells Muḥammad, *ṣalla Allāhu 'alayhi wa sallam*, that He has not left him and promises that things will be better in the future:

In the Name of Allah, the
Supremely Merciful, the Most
Kind.
By the glorious morning light,
And by the night
When it is still,
Thy Lord has not forsaken you,
Nor is He displeased.
And verily the Hereafter
Will be better for you
Than the present.
And soon will your Lord give
you (all good)
Then you shall be well-pleased.
Did He not find you an orphan
and give you shelter (and care)?
And He found you wandering,
and He gave you guidance.
And He found you in need, and
made you independent.
Therefore, treat not the orphan
with harshness.
Nor repulse the one who asks
But the Bounty of your Lord—
Rehearse and proclaim.

[Sūrah aḍ-Ḍuḥā (93): 1-11]

ط

إِنَّ ٱلَّذِينَ كَفَرُوا۟ وَصَدُّوا۟ عَن
سَبِيلِ ٱللَّهِ قَدْ ضَلُّوا۟ ضَلَٰلًۢا
بَعِيدًا ۝ إِنَّ ٱلَّذِينَ كَفَرُوا۟ وَظَلَمُوا۟
لَمْ يَكُنِ ٱللَّهُ لِيَغْفِرَ لَهُمْ وَلَا
لِيَهْدِيَهُمْ طَرِيقًا ۝ إِلَّا طَرِيقَ
جَهَنَّمَ خَٰلِدِينَ فِيهَآ أَبَدًا ۚ
وَكَانَ ذَٰلِكَ عَلَى ٱللَّهِ يَسِيرًا ۝

Those who reject Faith and keep (people) off from the way of Allah, have verily strayed far, far away from the path. Those who reject Faith and do wrong, Allah will not forgive them nor guide them to any way. Except the way of Hell, to stay therein forever; and this to Allah is easy.

[Sūrah an-Nisā' (4): 167-169]

ṬAREEQ

Ṭareeq is the Arabic word for a 'road' or a 'pathway'. If a person wants to go somewhere he will usually try to find the best way to get there; he will look for a way with the least turnings and as few ups and downs as possible. People can easily get lost if they don't know the way, and that's what happens on the road of life: many people think that they can guide themselves to happiness, they make up their own rules about life and even make up their own religions—these people go far astray.

Allah the Almighty has shown us the straightest path to reach the Garden of peace and happiness and He has warned us not to get lost. He has sent us Messengers whom we can trust; if we follow them then we will surely be guided right. But if we listen to the wrong kind of people they will mislead us and at the end of life's journey we would be very sorry indeed.

We must also be very careful to follow the signs which guide us on the road. Sometimes in life Allah commands us to stop what we're doing because we have to pray and remember Him, so too when we see the sign on the highway that says 'Stop' we must beware in case of danger. When we see a road-sign showing a picture of two old people, we must go slow and be careful; Allah the Almighty has commanded us to look after our parents – do we look after them as we should? Are we kind to them? Or do we rush past them sometimes even knocking them over? Allah forbid! Signs are there to guide us on the road; if we read the Book of Allah it is full of Signs showing us exactly the right way to go in true life.

Where are you going,
Where are you going,
North, South, East or the West?
Where are you headed,
Oh, where are you headed?
Turn to Allah, that's the best;
'Cause He is there, wherever you are
So turn, turn, turn to Allah

Where do you live,
Oh, where do you live,
In a tent or in a town?
It doesn't matter where you live,
you can soon be found;
'Cause He is there, wherever you are
So turn, turn, turn to Allah

Allāhu, Allāhu, Jalla Jalāluhu

ẒILL

ظ

Ẓill means a 'shadow' in Arabic. Shadows are made when light shines on one side of an object, creating a space of darkness behind it. Shadows give movement and life to everything; even things like mountains, houses and trees bow down to Allah Almighty. As their shadows move from right to left, morning and evening, they humbly join the creation in glorifying their Lord and Sustainer; praising Allah the Most High, as they all prostrate in line together.

Shadows are one of the signs of Allah to make us think and be grateful. When it's a very hot day we look for a shady place to escape from the sun's burning heat. This usually happens at *Ẓuhr*, midday, when the sun is high above our heads and shadows are smallest. As the day passes by, shadows get longer, stretching out more and more as the afternoon unfolds, making everything cooler and comfortable.

If there were no shadows, think how difficult life would be: sunbeams would bounce everywhere. You would have to close the windows and stay indoors until the sun went down, then it would be too dark to go out and do anything. Umbrellas wouldn't give shade and people would have to wear lots of tight clothes to avoid getting burnt. Everywhere would be similar – cold countries would become hotter because they would no longer be in the distant shadows of the sun. We thank Allah for the mercy of shadows and pray to be under the shade of His Throne on the Day of Judgement – when there will be no other shade.

أَوَلَمۡ يَرَوۡاْ إِلَىٰ مَا خَلَقَ ٱللَّهُ مِن شَيۡءٖ
يَتَفَيَّؤُاْ ظِلَٰلُهُۥ عَنِ ٱلۡيَمِينِ
وَٱلشَّمَآئِلِ سُجَّدٗا لِّلَّهِ وَهُمۡ دَٰخِرُونَ ۝
وَلِلَّهِ يَسۡجُدُ مَا فِي ٱلسَّمَٰوَٰتِ وَمَا فِي
ٱلۡأَرۡضِ مِن دَآبَّةٖ وَٱلۡمَلَٰٓئِكَةُ
وَهُمۡ لَا يَسۡتَكۡبِرُونَ ۝

Have they not observed all things that Allah has created, how their shadows incline to the right and left, making prostration to Allah in humility?

To Allah prostrates everything that is in the heavens and every creature crawling on the earth and the angels, and they are not proud.

[Sūrah an-Naḥl (16): 48-49]

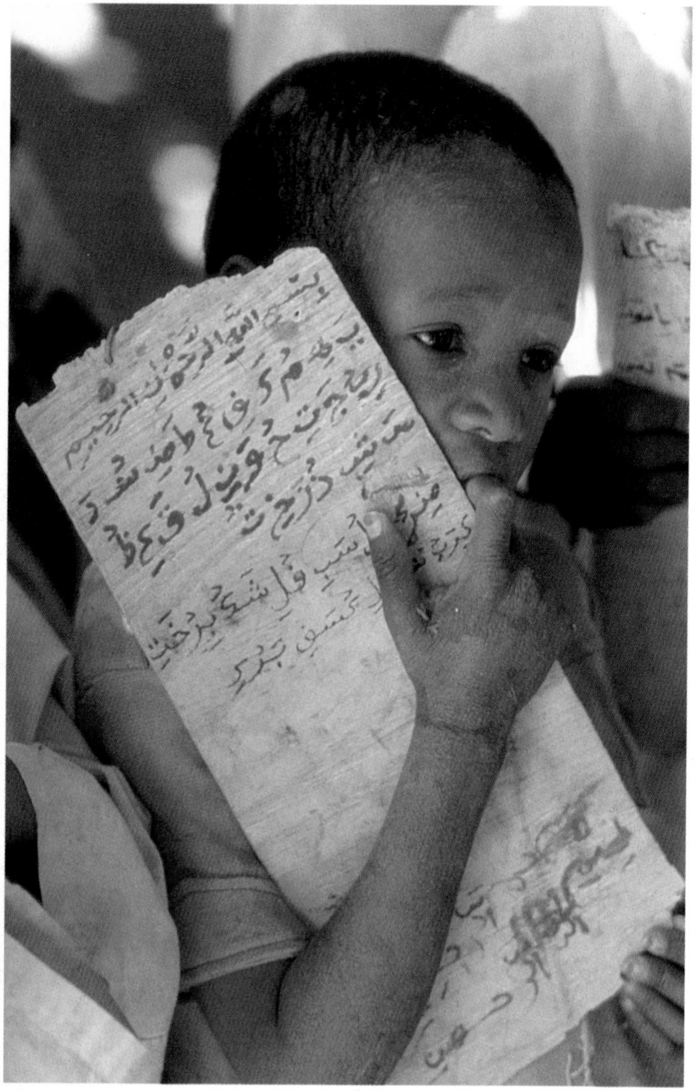

ع ‘ILM

‘Ilm is the Arabic word for knowledge. It is a duty on all Muslims to educate themselves so that they may gain knowledge. The first word revealed to the prophet Muḥammad, *ṣalla Allāhu ‘alayhi wa sallam*, was: ‘READ!’ Reading is one of the best ways to gain knowledge.

We read in the Qur’an that in the beginning, when the first man Adam was created, God blew of His Spirit into him and gave him his senses. Then, the first thing that he was taught was to know the ‘Names of all things.’ The angels were then ordered by Allah to bow down before Adam: this means that, if understood correctly, knowledge raises a human being to a higher position than other creatures of creation. Because of knowledge, man can gain wisdom, and that is one of the greatest gifts a person can have. Wisdom gives you the ability to know right from wrong; it is like a light which allows you to see in the darkness. When people are lost in ignorance and going astray, the person with knowledge becomes a beacon of light; he shines out amongst the rest and shows them the way to safety.

Another word for *'Ilm* is 'Science'. Today, there are many scientists spending a lifetime learning about the way the world works, looking into space and into microscopes, making new things, new modes of travel, new ways to communicate and speak to each other: computers, TV. But unfortunately, much of this type of knowledge is without guidance; it does not necessarily tell you what is good or bad. Some scientists are really quite silly: for example, a number of scientists think that because monkeys and chimpanzees have two arms, two legs and a small brain, that they must be just another type of humankind! They make up all sorts of stories, and draw pictures to make people believe what they say. They don't seem to know that all human beings belong to one special family. All of us are the children of Adam, and the angels would never bow down to a monkey — Allah forbid! That shows you that unless you have wisdom, you may not be able to judge what is right or wrong, what is true or false; this is the best knowledge which was given to the Prophets, *'alayhimu as-salām*.

وَقُل رَّبِّ زِدْنِي عِلْمًا

بِسۡمِ ٱللَّهِ ٱلرَّحۡمَٰنِ ٱلرَّحِيمِ

الٓمٓ ◇ ذَٰلِكَ ٱلۡكِتَٰبُ لَا رَيۡبَۛ
فِيهِۛ هُدٗى لِّلۡمُتَّقِينَ ◇ ٱلَّذِينَ يُؤۡمِنُونَ
بِٱلۡغَيۡبِ وَيُقِيمُونَ ٱلصَّلَوٰةَ وَمِمَّا رَزَقۡنَٰهُمۡ
يُنفِقُونَ ◇ وَٱلَّذِينَ يُؤۡمِنُونَ بِمَآ أُنزِلَ
إِلَيۡكَ وَمَآ أُنزِلَ مِن قَبۡلِكَ وَبِٱلۡأٓخِرَةِ
هُمۡ يُوقِنُونَ ◇ أُوْلَٰٓئِكَ عَلَىٰ هُدٗى
مِّن رَّبِّهِمۡۖ وَأُوْلَٰٓئِكَ هُمُ
ٱلۡمُفۡلِحُونَ ◆

GHAYB

Ghayb means the Unseen. To believe in the *Ghayb* is an important part of Faith. A Muslim must believe in certain unseen things: in Allah, the Lord of the Heavens and the earth; in His Angels; His Books of Revelation; in His Messengers; in *Qadar,* whatever will be – the good and bad; in the Life after death; the Last Day; and in Paradise and Hellfire. Looking around we can't see any of these things except the last Book of Allah, the Qur'an.

Even in this world there are many things which we don't see, but we know that they're there such as the air that we breath – without it we couldn't stay alive. Gravity makes things fall to the earth, but we can't see gravity itself. Everyone knows what love feels like, but you can't see or touch it.

People who don't believe in the Unseen, don't believe in Allah and the Last Day: they are blind to the Truth. However, if scientists give the news that a large meteorite is heading direct for the earth from outer space, most people would immediately believe them, even though they couldn't see it; they would hide in their homes and tremble with fear. Yet when the Qur'an tells them about Paradise and the punishment of the blazing Fire, they turn away in disbelief and say, 'But we can't see them.' It's as if they are in the dark; because they have no Faith, they cannot see the reality around them. But for those with Faith, everything is bright and clear.

غ

Allah says in His Noble Book:

In the name of Allah, the Supremely Merciful, the Most Kind. *Alif, Lām, Meem.* That is the Book, without doubt therein, a Guidance for those who are aware. Those who believe in the Unseen and establish Prayer and from out of what We have provided they spend. Those who believe in what was revealed to you (o Muḥammad) and what was revealed before you and about the Hereafter they are sure. Those are upon Guidance from their Lord and they are the successful.

[Sūrah al-Baqarah (2): 1-5]

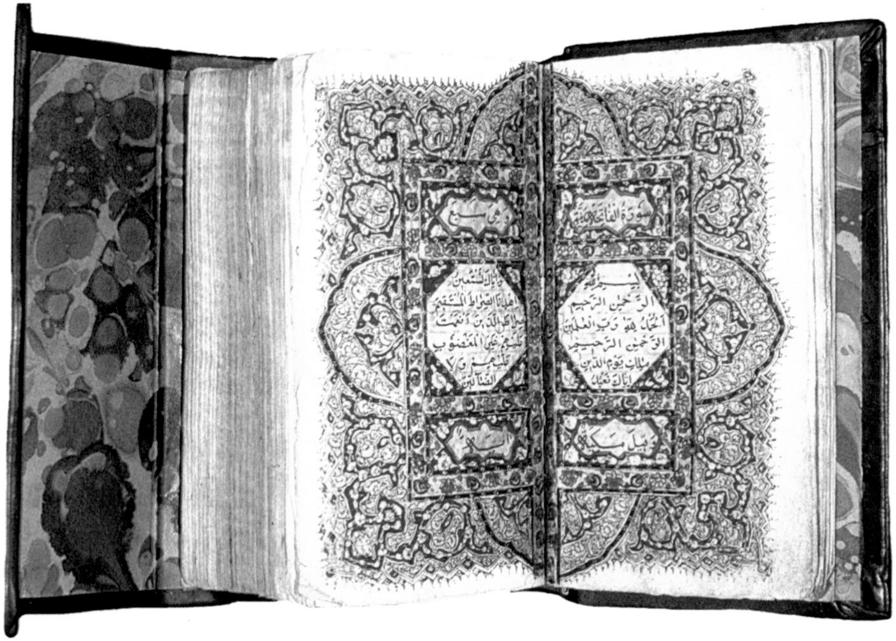

ف

FĀTIḤAH

Al-Fātiḥah means 'The Opening'. It is the first chapter of the Qur'an and is so important that it has been called the 'Mother of the Book' because it comes before all the other Sūrahs of the Qur'an and contains the meaning of everything that follows it. A Muslim will recite it every day in every Prayer.

بِسْمِ ٱللَّهِ ٱلرَّحْمَٰنِ ٱلرَّحِيمِ
ٱلْحَمْدُ لِلَّهِ رَبِّ ٱلْعَٰلَمِينَ ◇
ٱلرَّحْمَٰنِ ٱلرَّحِيمِ ◇ مَٰلِكِ يَوْمِ ٱلدِّينِ ◇
إِيَّاكَ نَعْبُدُ وَإِيَّاكَ نَسْتَعِينُ ◇ ٱهْدِنَا
ٱلصِّرَٰطَ ٱلْمُسْتَقِيمَ ◇ صِرَٰطَ ٱلَّذِينَ أَنْعَمْتَ
عَلَيْهِمْ غَيْرِ ٱلْمَغْضُوبِ عَلَيْهِمْ
وَلَا ٱلضَّآلِّينَ ◆ آمِينْ

This is an English translation of *Al-Fātiḥah*:

In the Name of Allah,
the Supremely Merciful, the Most Kind
Praise be to Allah,
Lord of all the worlds.
The Supremely Merciful, the Most Kind.
Master of the Day of Judgement
You alone do we worship
And You alone do we ask for help.
Guide us on the Straight Path.
The Path of those whom
You have favoured
Not the path of those
who have earned Your anger
Nor of those who have gone astray.

These few words are the essence of the Qur'an, containing the most important message of Islam. It begins with the name of Allah and then mentions His qualities, the first of which is His Mercy. Its words remind us how much we should praise Him; it reminds us that He is the Lord, the Owner of everything in this universe, the Supreme Authority Who is the most Just. One day we will all be standing in front of Him to be judged. This Sūrah teaches us that all our prayers and hopes are for Allah alone. Finally, we ask to be shown the right path, we express our wish to be included in the group who throughout the ages were blessed by Allah, and beg not to be included in the group who earn His anger or those who have lost their way.

Al-Fātiḥah is also a *du'ā*, a prayer which can be read almost anytime. It is the most complete prayer. It is wise to understand the words of *Al-Fātiḥah* in our hearts, so that it's meaning is always clear to us.

ق

QUR'AN

The *Qur'an* is the last Book of Allah. It was revealed to the Prophet Muḥammad, *ṣalla Allāhu 'alayhi wa sallam,* over a period of 23 years. The Qur'an is different from every other book in this world because it is the only one that was not the work of any human being. Allah the Almighty has revealed other Books to us, such as the Torah of Moses; the Psalms of David; and the Gospel given to Jesus, peace be upon them all. But these scriptures have all been changed by people in one way or another since they were revealed, leaving the Qur'an as the last Word – unchanged – and the only sure guidance from Allah.

The Qur'an was revealed to Prophet Muḥammad, *ṣalla Allāhu 'alayhi wa sallam,* who could neither read nor write. It was first brought by the Angel Gabriel during a night in Ramaḍān while Muḥammad, *ṣalla Allāhu 'alayhi wa sallam,* was in retreat in a cave on Mount Ḥirā, just outside Makkah.

The Qur'an is written in the most beautiful Arabic and in it we can find guidance about everything in life. It teaches us the laws we have to live by and lessons about people who lived before us. It tells us about the many Prophets and Messengers who were sent to show people the straight path. The most important message it brings us is the Truth about God Himself, the way we must obey Him, and how we can come closer to Him. The Qur'an warns us about the greatest sin: to believe or imagine that there is any other god beside Him.

Many lucky people know the Qur'an by heart, even though it is very long. There are one hundred and fourteen Sūrahs, or chapters, and in each Sūrah, a number of Ayahs. The Prophet Muḥammad, *ṣalla Allāhu 'alayhi wa sallam,* said, 'The best of you is he who learns the Qur'an and then teaches it to others.'[10] As Muslims, we should try to read and understand the Qur'an before anything else. We know for sure that it is the true guidance from Allah, so we must try to be best, like the Prophet, *ṣalla Allāhu 'alayhi wa sallam,* said.

Qur'ānu Rabbee, Qur'ānu Rabbee
Huddan wa nūrun li-kulli qalbee

Muḥammadun jā'a bi-ar-risālah
Yusabbiḥu-Allāha Dha-al-jalālah
Fa-baddada-al-Kufra wa-ad-dalālah
Bi-mā hawāhu, Qur'ānu Rabbee

Qur'ānu Rabbee, Qur'ānu Rabbee
Huddan wa nūrun li-kulli qalbee

Qur'ānu Rabbee li-an-nāsi bushrā
Wa raḥmatun li-al-'ibādi zukhrā
Wa feehi li-al-mu'mineena dhikrā
Wa feehi yusrun, Qur'ānu Rabbee

بِسْمِ ٱللَّهِ ٱلرَّحْمَٰنِ ٱلرَّحِيمِ
إِنَّآ أَنزَلْنَٰهُ فِى لَيْلَةِ ٱلْقَدْرِ ۝ وَمَآ أَدْرَىٰكَ
مَا لَيْلَةُ ٱلْقَدْرِ ۝ لَيْلَةُ ٱلْقَدْرِ خَيْرٌ مِّنْ أَلْفِ
شَهْرٍ ۝ تَنَزَّلُ ٱلْمَلَٰٓئِكَةُ وَٱلرُّوحُ فِيهَا بِإِذْنِ
رَبِّهِم مِّن كُلِّ أَمْرٍ ۝ سَلَٰمٌ هِىَ حَتَّىٰ مَطْلَعِ ٱلْفَجْرِ

In the name of Allah, The Supremely Merciful, Most Kind.
Verily We sent it down in the Night of Power. And what will convey to you what the Night of Power is? The Night of Power is better than a thousand months. In it the angels descended as did the Spirit, by the permission of their Lord on every affair. Peace – this, until the rising of the dawn.

[Ṣurah al-Qadr (97):1-5]

أَلَمْ تَرَ كَيْفَ ضَرَبَ ٱللَّهُ مَثَلًا كَلِمَةً طَيِّبَةً كَشَجَرَةٍ طَيِّبَةٍ أَصْلُهَا ثَابِتٌ وَفَرْعُهَا فِى ٱلسَّمَآءِ ◇ تُؤْتِى أُكُلَهَا كُلَّ حِينٍ بِإِذْنِ رَبِّهَا وَيَضْرِبُ ٱللَّهُ ٱلْأَمْثَالَ لِلنَّاسِ لَعَلَّهُمْ يَتَذَكَّرُونَ ◇ وَمَثَلُ كَلِمَةٍ خَبِيثَةٍ كَشَجَرَةٍ خَبِيثَةٍ ٱجْتُثَّتْ مِن فَوْقِ ٱلْأَرْضِ مَا لَهَا مِن قَرَارٍ ◆

KALIMAH

ك

Kalimah means a 'Saying' or a 'Word' and is mentioned many times in the Qur'an. People should be extra careful about what they say and what words they use, because it is the chief thing that can either lead them closer to Heaven or push them nearer towards the Fire. The Prophet Muḥammad, *ṣalla Allahu 'alayhi wa sallam,* said, 'Guard yourselves against the Fire of Hell even if it be with only half a date given in charity; and if one cannot afford that then, at least, he should speak a good word.'[11]

So to speak a polite word can be the same as giving help to the needy; and it is a treasure which even poor people can use if they've got nothing else to give away in charity. If a person cannot say anything good then perhaps it's better for him to keep silent; that's better than vain and worthless talk. The worse kind of words are those which carry lies and stories behind people's backs – and the most evil of them is the word of *Kufr,* or rejection of Allah.

Do you not see how Allah strikes for you a similitude? - a goodly word is like a goodly tree, whose root is firmly fixed, and its branches reach to the heavens;

It brings forth fruit at all times, by the permission of its Lord. Allah strikes forth similitudes for people, in order that they may be reminded.

And the similitude of an evil word is that of an evil tree: it is torn up by its root from the surface of the earth; it has no stability.

[Sūrah Ibrāhīm (14): 24-26]

11 Al-Bukhari and Muslim (Riyāḍ aṣ-Ṣaliheen no. 696)

لا إله إلا الله محمد رسول الله

LĀ ILĀHA ILLA-ALLĀH

Lā illāha illa-Allah means, 'There is no God except Allah'. It is the most important thing for every person to know; and no one can be a Muslim without fully believing in the Oneness of Allah. The Prophet Muḥammad, *ṣalla Allāhu 'alayhi wa sallam,* said that whoever died knowing that there is no God except Allah shall enter Paradise.[12] Of course, once a person has accepted the truth, only then will he be asked to complete the other articles of faith, otherwise he'll be declared a non-Muslim or *kāfir* if he has rejected it.

The Kalimah, *'Lā illāha illa-Allāh'*, helps us to understand the Unity behind all things – seen or unseen – in this great universe. Allah caused all things to exist: He is the Creator of everything. All the Prophets of God who were sent to this world taught the people this same basic message, so that they would come together and worship the One true Lord of all creation. Unfortunately, some people refused to listen so they created false gods and changed their original Religion. They could not have done this if Allah had not given them the choice and ability to do so; He is the Almighty and has power over everything.

Allah has the most beautiful names, each of them describes His eternal attributes: for example, He is *'Al-Awwal'* – the First, which means that Allah, *subhānahu wa ta'ālā*, was before everything else, when nothing else existed. A person may be first in class or in a race but he can never be the first before everything; that is why Allah's names are not the same as anyone or anything found in creation.

We only need to call upon Him in our prayers; we don't need saints or special people to carry our prayers up to heaven and we don't have to raise our voices either because Allah Almighty hears and sees all things. The Prophet Muḥammad, *ṣalla Allāhu 'alayhi wa sallam,* said, 'Allah, Great and Glorious, has ninety-nine names, one hundred minus one, and whoever memorizes their number will enter Paradise'.[13] Therefore, whoever believes that there is no God but Allah, and calls on Him by His names, will understand the Oneness of God – *at-Tawḥeed*.

هُوَ ٱللَّهُ ٱلَّذِى لَآ إِلَٰهَ إِلَّا هُوَ ۖ عَٰلِمُ
ٱلْغَيْبِ وَٱلشَّهَٰدَةِ ۖ هُوَ ٱلرَّحْمَٰنُ
ٱلرَّحِيمُ ۝ هُوَ ٱللَّهُ ٱلَّذِى
لَآ إِلَٰهَ إِلَّا هُوَ ٱلْمَلِكُ ٱلْقُدُّوسُ
ٱلسَّلَٰمُ ٱلْمُؤْمِنُ ٱلْمُهَيْمِنُ
ٱلْعَزِيزُ ٱلْجَبَّارُ ٱلْمُتَكَبِّرُ ۚ
سُبْحَٰنَ ٱللَّهِ عَمَّا يُشْرِكُونَ ۝
هُوَ ٱللَّهُ ٱلْخَٰلِقُ ٱلْبَارِئُ
ٱلْمُصَوِّرُ ۖ لَهُ ٱلْأَسْمَآءُ ٱلْحُسْنَىٰ ۚ
يُسَبِّحُ لَهُۥ مَا فِى ٱلسَّمَٰوَٰتِ
وَٱلْأَرْضِ ۖ وَهُوَ ٱلْعَزِيزُ ٱلْحَكِيمُ ۝

He is Allah, there is no God but He: Knower of (all things) secret and open; He is the Supremely Merciful, the Most Kind.

He is Allah, there is no God but He: the King, the Most Holy, the Giver of Peace, the Faithful, the Guardian, the Exalted in Might, the Irresistible, the Proud: glory to Allah! (high is He) above what they associate with Him.

He is the Creator, the Originator, the Fashioner. To Him belong the most beautiful names. All that is in the heavens and earth glorifies Him; and He is the Exalted in Might, the Most Wise.

[Sūrah al-Ḥashr (59): 22-24]

12 Ṣaḥeeḥ Muslim 13 Al-Bukhari and Muslim (Mishkāt al-Maṣābeeḥ vol. 3, ch. 38, p. 736)

م

MUḤAMMAD RASŪL-ALLĀH

Muḥammad Rasūl-Allāh is the second part of the *Kalimah* that someone must believe and say to become a Muslim: it means, 'Muḥammad is the Messenger of Allah'.

Muḥammad, *ṣalla Allāhu 'alayhi wa sallam,* was sent by Allah as the Last Prophet for all mankind; he was given the Qur'an, which made clear what others Prophets and Messengers had said before him, inviting people to the Oneness of God. His life was a perfect model of Faith and he brought the final rules of God's Religion – *al-Islām*.

Muḥammad, *ṣalla Allāhu 'alayhi wa sallam,* was born in Makkah from the family line of the Prophet Abraham, *'alayhi al-salām*; he belonged to the famous tribe of Hashim. Even before being appointed as the Messenger, people used to love and respect Muḥammad, *ṣalla Allāhu 'alayhi wa sallam,* for his wonderful and kind character; he always looked after the poor and was the most trusted person. At the age of forty he received the first words of the Qur'an from Angel Gabriel. From then on, he delivered the message of Islam to mankind – as he received it – faithfully. His is the most amazing story: Muḥammad's life, *ṣalla Allāhu 'alayhi wa sallam,* and his community of followers, became shaped and guided by the flow of Revelations which descended from heaven. Gradually, the enemies of Islam, after trying their best to defeat and destroy the Religion, gave up. Victory came with the liberation of Makkah from the evil grip of the idol-worshippers; God's House – the Holy Ka'bah – was cleansed and Islam's light began to spread throughout the world. Muḥammad, *ṣalla Allāhu 'alayhi wa sallam,* died at the age of sixty-three in Madeenah not long after performing his farewell pilgrimage. His grave can still be visited, and to this day, millions of Muslims from all over the world travel to pay their respects and give salutations to the beloved Prophet. May Allah bless him and grant him eternal safety and peace and raise him to the loftiest place in heaven.

Because everything Muḥammad, *ṣalla Allāhu 'alayhi wa sallam,* said and did has been recorded so perfectly in the Qur'an and the books of his sayings – *Aḥādeeth* – we know enough about his life to be able to try and follow his example step by step. By doing this we can learn how to think and behave in the right way as true believers following the Religion of Truth.

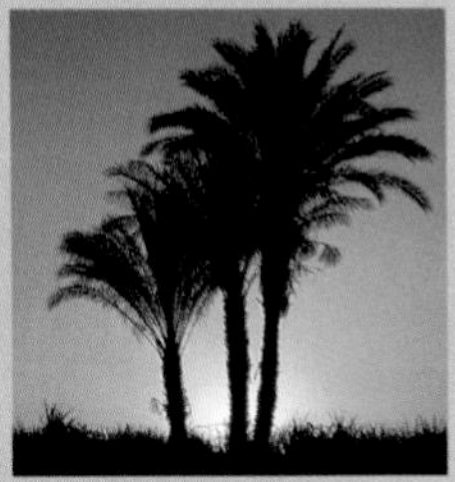

Salla-Allāhu 'alā Muḥammad
Salla-Allāh 'alaihi wa sallam
Salla-Allāhu 'alā Muḥammad
Salla-Allāh 'alaihi wa sallam

He was a guide for all people,
And a Mercy to the universe,
Was a guide for all people:
God's peace and blessings on him.

Salla-Allāhu 'alā Muḥammad
Salla-Allāh 'alaihi wa sallam

He was a seal of the Prophets,
The last brick in the house
of Prophethood;
He was the last of the Prophets.
God's peace and blessings on him.

Salla-Allāhu 'alā Muḥammad
Salla-Allāh 'alaihi wa sallam

He was a patron of the poor;
Always helping widows and orphans,
A great patron of the poor:
God's peace and blessings on him.

Salla-Allāhu 'alā Muḥammad
Salla-Allāh 'alaihi wa sallam

He was a striver against evil,
And he fought - and he won,
To give rights to all people:
God's peace and blessings on him.

Salla-Allāhu 'alā Muḥammad
Salla-Allāh 'alaihi wa sallam

He was a stranger to this world,
For his aim was the Hereafter;
He cared little for this world:
God's peace and blessings on him.

Salla-Allāhu 'alā Muḥammad
Salla-Allāh 'alaihi wa sallam

NAWM

ن

Nawm is the Arabic for sleep, something that all creatures need. Only Allah the Almighty is not in need of sleep: He is *Al-Qayyūm*, the Self-Sustaining; He takes no rest — never at all, otherwise everything in this universe would disappear in a blink of an eye.

Allah created sleep as a gift and a comfort for us. People, creatures and plants all enjoy a time of rest: in winter, the fields and the forests of the earth go to sleep, in spring they wake up again. Sleep is also a little like dying: when we lie down in bed, it reminds us how one day we will be laid in our graves. Therefore, it's always important to remember the name of Allah when going to sleep: the Prophet, *ṣalla Allāhu 'alayhi wa sallam,* used to say, 'In Your name o Allah, I die and I live'.[14] So each day we arise from our beds is like a resurrection. We should be reminded by this, that our life on earth is a short one, from which we will one day wake up in the Hereafter.

The Prophet Muḥammad, *ṣalla Allāhu 'alayhi wa sallam,* often spent much of the night in prayer whilst others were sleeping. He recommended this as one of the best times to pray and communicate with the Lord of the worlds. It also shows that we are prepared to sacrifice the comfort of sleep in order to gain the pleasure of Allah.

تَتَجَافَىٰ جُنُوبُهُمْ عَنِ الْمَضَاجِعِ
يَدْعُونَ رَبَّهُمْ خَوْفًا وَطَمَعًا وَمِمَّا
رَزَقْنَاهُمْ يُنفِقُونَ ۝ فَلَا تَعْلَمُ نَفْسٌ
مَّا أُخْفِيَ لَهُم مِّن قُرَّةِ أَعْيُنٍ جَزَاءً
بِمَا كَانُوا يَعْمَلُونَ ۝

In Sūrah *As-Sajdah* (Prostration), verse sixteen, Allah says:

They leave their beds to call on their Lord in fear and hope: and they spend from what We have provided for them.

So no person knows what delights of the eye are kept hidden for them as a reward for their deeds.

[Sūrah as-Sajdah (32): 16]

14 Al-Bukhari

ه HIJRAH

Hijrah is emigration, which means leaving home and moving to another country or place to make a new home there. But *Hijrah* in Islam is a special kind of emigration: it doesn't mean just moving somewhere to find work and make money, or be near family and friends – it means to leave your home for the sake of Allah.

The Islamic calendar began from the year Prophet Muḥammad, *ṣalla Allāhu 'alayhi wa sallam,* emigrated to Madeenah. After declaring Islam to the people of Makkah, he and his followers were mistreated by them. Some were tortured or even killed. Many of the Companions were poor and were not protected by belonging to strong and powerful families, so Muḥammad, *ṣalla Allāhu 'alayhi wa sallam,* allowed about one hundred of them to make *Hijrah* to Abyssinia (now called Ethiopia) which was ruled by a good Christian king. The Quraish, the most powerful tribe in Makkah, tried to bring them back, but they didn't succeed; the King treated them fairly and gave them the right to stay and practice their religion. So he was the first King to accept Islam.

There were more and more plots to destroy Islam; life became more and more difficult for Muslims in Makkah. People from the city of Yathrib invited Muḥammad, *ṣalla Allāhu 'alayhi wa sallam,* to come and be their ruler and to help settle the arguments between the people there. So the Muslims emigrated there little by little. When our Prophet Muḥammad, *ṣalla Allāhu 'alayhi wa sallam,* arrived, the city was renamed *Madeenah an Nabee* – the City of the Prophet. These Muslims were called the *Muhajirun* – the emigrants. They had to give up a lot of wealth and possessions when they migrated to Madeenah. This leads us to the Islamic meaning of the word *Hijrah*: to give up the things that we love for the sake of Allah.

It is said that when Muḥammad, *ṣalla Allāhu 'alayhi wa sallam,* travelled with his companion Abu Bakr across the mountains and desert towards Madeenah, the enemies sent horsemen to kill them. But they took refuge in a cave. The horsemen came to the cave, but when they saw that a spider had spun a web across the entrance and that a dove sat undisturbed nearby, they thought that there can be nobody inside, so they left and went away.

Many Prophets including Ibrāhīm (Abraham), Lūṭ (Lot) and Mūsā (Moses) made *Hijrah* for the sake of their religion. Sūrah *as-Ṣāffāt* (the Ranks), verse ninety-nine tells of Ibrāhīm's faith in Allah, when he was leaving home he said:

> I will go to my Lord; He will surely guide me

Also we read about the *Hijrah* of the Prophet Lūṭ when he was told by the angels to leave his town he said:

> I will leave my home for the sake of my Lord, for He is Exalted in Might, Wise.[15]

These examples show us how we must be prepared, if necessary, to leave everything that we have in order to show our greater love for Allah. To do this shows complete trust in Allah, and we can be sure that He will reward us for doing so.

15 [Sūrah al-'Ankabūt (29): 26]

WUḌŪ'

Wuḍū' is the way of washing the body that Muslims do before making *Ṣalāh* (Prayers). In the same way as *Zakah* cleans and purifies our wealth, so *wuḍū'* cleans and purifies our bodies. By making *wuḍū'* we also make ourselves spiritually clean, so that we may be in a fit state to pray; without *wuḍū'* a person cannot make *Ṣalāh.* In Sūrah *Al-Ma'idah* (the Table Spread), verse six, Allah Almighty tells us:

> 'O you who believe, when you rise up for prayer, wash your faces and your hands to the elbows; and wipe your heads and your feet to the ankles…'

The parts of the body that we have to wash before *Ṣalāh* are those that can easily become dusty and dirty; those places like the head, the hands and feet also touch the floor of the Mosque, so they should be clean. In the country or desert, if there is no water to wash with, then pure sand or earth can be used to wipe the face and hands. Being clean is so important for a Muslim that it is mentioned in one of the first revelations given by Allah to Muḥammad, *ṣalla Allāhu 'alayhi wa sallam.*

Elsewhere in the Qur'an it says that, "Allah surely loves those who very often turn to Him, and He loves those who purify themselves."[16]

بِسْمِ ٱللَّهِ ٱلرَّحْمَٰنِ ٱلرَّحِيمِ

يَٰٓأَيُّهَا ٱلْمُدَّثِّرُ ۝ قُمْ فَأَنذِرْ ۝

وَرَبَّكَ فَكَبِّرْ ۝ وَثِيَابَكَ فَطَهِّرْ ۝

وَٱلرُّجْزَ فَٱهْجُرْ ۝

O you wrapped up
(in a mantle)!
Arise and deliver
your warning!
And magnify your Lord!
And keep your clothes free
from stains; and stay away from
pollution.

[Sūrah al-Muddaththir (74): 1-5]

Prophet Muḥammad, *ṣalla Allāhu 'alayhi wa sallam,* said: 'Cleanliness is half of the Faith.'[17] He taught us the right way to make *wuḍū'*, so that we not only clean our bodies, but also wash away our sins.

16 Sūrah al-Baqarah (2) : 222 17 Ṣaḥeeḥ Muslim (also Mishkāt al-Maṣābeeḥ, vol. 1, ch. 7, p. 663)

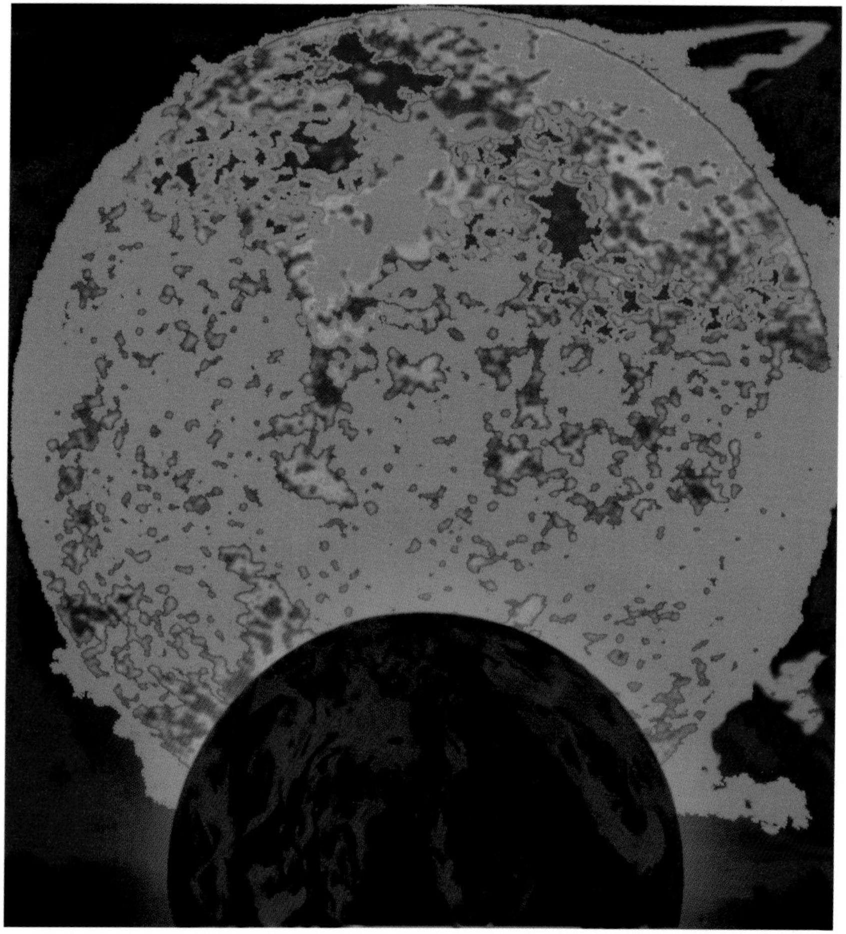

YAWM AD-DEEN

ي

Yawm ad-Deen is the Day of Judgement. All people have been given guidance – at one time or another – about the right way to live; and each of us have been given a choice: whether we follow a good path or not. On the Day of Judgement, everything we ever thought, all actions, all movements, every word we ever said or heard, good and bad, will be presented to us in a Book. Even if we did things in secret, it makes no difference, because all things will be known by Allah Almighty. In the Sūrah called 'The Earthquake', it tells us, 'Whoever has done an atom's weight of good shall see it; and whoever has done an atom's weight of evil shall see it (also).'[18] This teaches us that we must always keep *Yawm ad-Deen* present in our hearts and minds, so if we ever do something wrong, we should feel sorry, repent and try hard to go back to the right path.

In this life it is sometimes difficult to see true justice and to know who is right and who is wrong, because the truth may be hidden, but on the Day of Judgement it will be seen and known for sure. *Yawm ad-Deen* is the Day all people will be sorted out into groups: the people of the Fire will be gathered and then led to the gates of Hell. They will be questioned harshly, then they will be told to enter. Also, the people of Paradise will be sorted into groups and then led to the gates of the Garden. There they will be welcomed with a greeting of 'Peace', and then they will be asked to enter.[19] This shows how the good will be separated from the bad on that Day so that we will clearly see and know the difference – and Allah alone is the Final Judge.

18 Sūrah az-Zalzalah (99): 7-8 19 Sūrah az-Zumar (39): 71-73

In the Name of Allah, the Supremely Merciful, the Most Kind.
When the sky is split apart; and when the stars are scattered; and when the seas burst forth; and when the graves are overturned – every human being will (at last) know what it has sent before and what it has held back. O Man! What has kept you away from your Lord the Most Generous? Who created you and shaped you and gave you (the measure of) what is just. In whatever shape He wished, He put you together. Nay! But you reject the Judgement! Yet truly over you are two protectors; Honoured, writing (down your deeds); They know all that you do. As for the righteous, they will be in bliss; and as for the wicked, they will be in the fire, which they will enter on the Day of Judgement, and they will not be allowed to be (kept) away from it. And what will explain to you what the Day of Judgement is? Again, what will explain to you what the Day of Judgement is? It will be the Day when no soul can help at all any other – for the Command that Day will be (wholly) for Allah.

[Sūrah al-Infiṭār (82): 1-19]

بِسْمِ ٱللَّهِ ٱلرَّحْمَٰنِ ٱلرَّحِيمِ

إِذَا ٱلسَّمَآءُ ٱنفَطَرَتْ ◇ وَإِذَا ٱلْكَوَاكِبُ ٱنتَثَرَتْ ◇ وَإِذَا ٱلْبِحَارُ
فُجِّرَتْ ◇ وَإِذَا ٱلْقُبُورُ بُعْثِرَتْ ◇ عَلِمَتْ نَفْسٌ مَّا قَدَّمَتْ
وَأَخَّرَتْ ◇ يَٰٓأَيُّهَا ٱلْإِنسَٰنُ مَا غَرَّكَ بِرَبِّكَ ٱلْكَرِيمِ ◇ ٱلَّذِى
خَلَقَكَ فَسَوَّىٰكَ فَعَدَلَكَ ◇ فِىٓ أَىِّ صُورَةٍ مَّا شَآءَ رَكَّبَكَ ◇
كَلَّا بَلْ تُكَذِّبُونَ بِٱلدِّينِ ◇ وَإِنَّ عَلَيْكُمْ لَحَٰفِظِينَ ◇ كِرَامًا
كَٰتِبِينَ ◇ يَعْلَمُونَ مَا تَفْعَلُونَ ◇ إِنَّ ٱلْأَبْرَارَ لَفِى نَعِيمٍ ◇ وَإِنَّ
ٱلْفُجَّارَ لَفِى جَحِيمٍ ◇ يَصْلَوْنَهَا يَوْمَ ٱلدِّينِ ◇ وَمَا هُمْ عَنْهَا بِغَآئِبِينَ ◇
وَمَآ أَدْرَىٰكَ مَا يَوْمُ ٱلدِّينِ ◇ ثُمَّ مَآ أَدْرَىٰكَ مَا يَوْمُ ٱلدِّينِ ◇
يَوْمَ لَا تَمْلِكُ نَفْسٌ لِّنَفْسٍ شَيْـًٔا ۖ وَٱلْأَمْرُ يَوْمَئِذٍ لِّلَّهِ ◆

Acknowledgements

Dr. Syed Mutawalli Darsh, Dr. Suhaib Hasan,
Imam Abdullah Zein Al-Abdin, Dr Muhammad Isa Waley,
Tayyib Rana, Khaleel Muhammad

Lyrics & Translations

Song translations: Yusuf Islam
Say He is Allah: Sarwar Rija
Qur'ānu Rabee: Samira Habashi

Calligraphy, Illustration & Photocollage

The name of Allah, p.8; Sūrah Yā-Seen p.22; Thawāb, p.13;
Deen (sidebar) p.21; Shams (sidebar) p.35; Yawm ad-Deen p.60.
All except p.8 & 22 by Abd al-Lateef Whiteman © 1999

Book Design

Abd al-Lateef Whiteman

Cover Art

Abd al-Lateef Whiteman & Yusuf Islam

Photography

Pages: 9, 10, 11,14,17(inset),18, 20, 22, 23, 28, 29, 32, 35, 37,
38, 40, 44, 46, 52-54, 56, 58: Peter Sanders Photography
Pages 16-17: Ovidio Salazar / Peter Sanders Photography
Page 8: Image Bank
Pages 24-25, 26, 31: Stockbyte
Page 30: By kind permission of The Bodleian Library (from Ibn ash-Shatir's book on the motions of the sun, moon and planets)

Project Manager

Tayyeb Shah

www.mountainoflight.com

ALSO FEATURING YUSUF ISLAM

A *is for* ALLAH

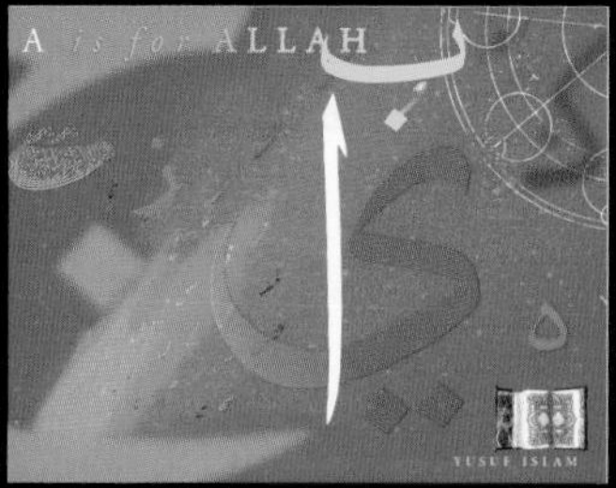

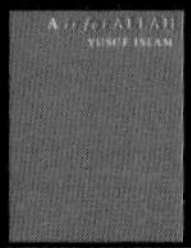

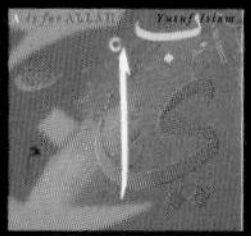

DOUBLE CASSETTE DOUBLE CD

It took 20 years for Yusuf Islam to develop *A is for Allah* from a song to a monumental and attractive work.

This book is also available on Double CD and Double Cassette and features:

- Complete book narrated by Yusuf Islam
- Qur'anic recitation by renowned Egyptian *Qari* Sheikh Muhammad Gibreel
- English translation read by Imam Hamza Yusuf from the USA
- 8 songs - 7 arranged & written by Yusuf Islam including the title track *A is for Allah* - and introducing Zain Bhikha from South Africa
- Guest appearance by Malaysia's world famous nasheed group Raihan performing harmonies on Yusuf's *Seal of The Prophets*
- Adhan by the Muazzin of Makkah

Approx. running time 101 minutes

Hardback Book · Double CD · Double Cassette
Cover Poster · A is for Allah Song Lyrics Poster
2 CD + Book & postcard pack
2 Cassette + Book & postcard pack

30th Juz *of the* Holy Qur'an

Arabic recitation by Sheikh Muhammad Al-Minyaoui
English narrated by Yusuf Islam

With Islam today having over one billion followers, the Qur'an is probably the most widely read book in the world, with sections of it being recited at least five times a day by Muslims during their daily prayers.

This recording features the original Arabic recited by the respected Egyptian *Qari* (reciter) Sheikh Muhammad Al-Minyaoui with each verse being followed by its English translation read by Yusuf Islam. The Arabic recitation style is *tartil* and the English narration is based upon *The Noble Qur'an* translated by Dr. Muhammad Taqi-ud-Din Al-Hilali and Dr. Muhammad Muhsin Khan.

Approx. running time 120 minutes

Double CD · Double Cassette

The Life of the Last Prophet ﷺ

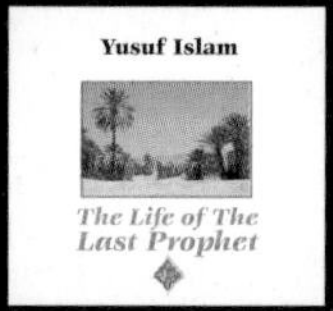

With over 350,000 copies sold, this spoken-word recording of the life of Prophet Muhammad ﷺ was the first official release by Yusuf Islam since his departure from the music business as Cat Stevens back in 1978. The biography is fully authenticated and approved by an international group of *'ulema* (scholars) and contains selected verses of the Qur'an, recited by the respected Egyptian *Qari* (reciter) Sheikh Muhammad Al-Minyaoui. It also includes the song *Tala'a al-Badru 'Alayna*, and a beautiful rendition of the *adhan* (call to prayer) and is the best concise biography on the Prophet Muhammad ﷺ available in English.

Approx. running time: 60 minutes

CD · Cassette · Hardback Book
Giftcase - Hardback Book + CD · Giftcase - Hardback Book + Cassette

Prayers of the Last Prophet ﷺ

Prayers of The Last Prophet ﷺ is the follow-up to the hugely successful *The Life of the Last Prophet* ﷺ, and contains a collection of *du'as* (supplications) as used by the Prophet Muhammad ﷺ. Narrated by Yusuf Islam and structured around phases of the day, these *du'as* cover a range of everyday activities seeking God's guidance. All are derived from Qur'an and Hadith and are fully authenticated. *Prayers* also contains Qur'anic recitation by the acclaimed Egyptian *Qari* (reciter) the late Sheikh Mahmoud Khalil Alhousari and features 3 new songs including Yusuf Islam's *If You Ask Me*.

Approx. running time: 60 minutes

CD · Cassette · Hardback Book
Giftcase - Hardback Book + CD · Giftcase - Hardback Book + Cassette

WELCOME TO THE QUR'AN
Gateway to Faith

This is the first in the Islamic Circle Talks series, adapted from talks given by Yusuf Islam at Regent's Park Mosque, London. Here, Yusuf takes the listener on a journey of discovery as he introduces the majestic beauty of the Qur'an through the gateway of faith. Includes Qur'anic recitation by Egyptian *Qari* Ahmed Ali Abd al-Tawab and nasheed *Qur'anu Rabbee*.

Approx. running time: 48 minutes
Cassette

The Prophetic Art of COMMUNICATION *Introduction to Da'wah*

Tape 2 in the Islamic Circle Talk series is about how the Prophets delivered God's message. This talk reminds us all of the importance of inviting people to Islam and particularly the methodology to use following the *sunnah* (example) of the last Prophet Muhammad ﷺ

Approx. running time: 39 minutes
Cassette

MOUNTAIN *of* LIGHT

[redacted]